Plant
this
Diamond

By

PAULETTE LEWIS-BROWN

authorHOUSE®

AuthorHouse™
1663 Liberty Drive
Bloomington, IN 47403
www.authorhouse.com
Phone: 1 (800) 839-8640

Published by AuthorHouse 04/04/2019

ISBN: 978-1-7283-0458-8 (sc)
ISBN: 978-1-7283-0457-1 (e)

Print information available on the last page.

This book is printed on acid-free paper.

CONTENTS

WORLD DIAMOND ◈

What if the world was

Filled with diamonds

With every heart open

Wide to pressurize them.

Would we share the love

That we feel for each

Other. Or could we guess

Who we are just to fit in.

Could we be sisters and

Brothers with the dna

Unknown yet we sparkle in

The squint of an eye◉

Smile and enjoy

Because you're a large

Piece of the diamond family pie.

Hats off to every mother

And father. ◈Diamonds are

 Forever◈. Settings dip in

Love to create the world

Largest diamond◈.

Look Deep In Your Heart ◆

Look deep in your heart

You will find me there

Look deep in your heart

Find the one who truly care.

Fun laughter and roses

A clue hiding behind the

Curtain with a suspense

Note that attached to the

Future. So the present is

Now, the past is lacking

Oxygen. Go ahead and

Dance like the farm man.

It's clear to see this from

The start.

Look deep in your heart

Show me your diamond

Thought.

Only The Winner Will Win.

Look Deep In Your Heart.

Show Me Your Art.

Keepsake 💎

Read Me First

Then Use Me Wisely.

Give Me A Room

Without A Gurney

Freedom To See An

Angel Without

Judging. Assume

Nothing. Just Use

Me Wisely Like A

Diamond 💎 Trophy 🏆.

In The End. Everyone

Will Be On The Same

Team. Keepsake Is Real.

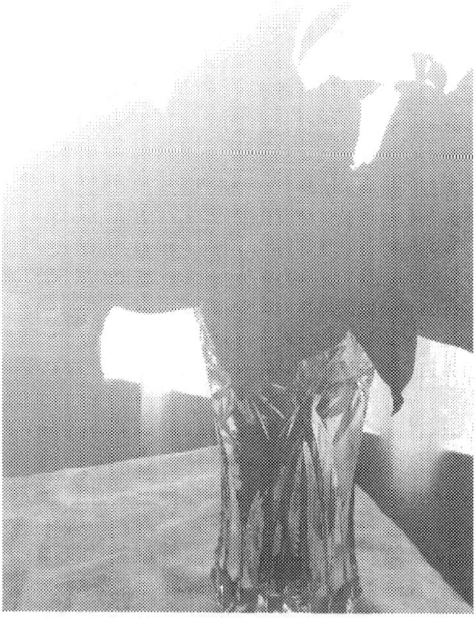

SILENT ROOM 💎

Work In A Silent Room.

One Script Will Not

Work For Everybody Zoom.

One For Males The Other

For The Ladies Bloom.

Stay Focus In The Midst Of

The Silent Clues.

Energy Is Important

You're Entering This Zone

Blindfolded. Harmony Is

Needed To Curve Ball The

Tension. Stay Away From

Distractions. Every Sale

Is On This Plant This

Diamond 💎 Scale.

I Can Just Imagine The

Nature In This Silent Room.

Weight Is Important News.

Chosen Few.

POSITIVE MINDS ♦

Positive Minds Will

Send Good People

Positive Vibes Will

Will Release The

Pressure.

Positive Life Will

Welcome More

Money To Feed

The Family Tree.

Positive Minds Will

Always Work Great

Together Feel Free.

Precious Diamonds ♦ 💍

Bond Forever In Every

Weather. Keep A Positive

Mind, For The Future.

ONE DIAMOND TWO BRAINS

Turn Me Into A Piece

Of Jamaican Diamond

With America On Top.

Share Me With All Your

Friends. See Who Would

Be Smart Enough To Keep

Me Close. Send My Mind A

Head Rest To Sensor Your

Diamond Research Test

See That This Gift Is No

Curse, Come On This Poem

Is Not The Worst.

Set A Diamond ♦ On My

Name. One Diamond Two

Queens.

WHICH WAY AM I GOING

Start On A Ledge

Work Your Way In.

Climb The Ladder To

Success. Yes You Can

Win. See No Evil Only

The One That Trust In

God Will Survive.

Moonwalk To The Line

Diamond Is Waiting On

The Sideline.

Straight And Narrow Was

The Only Base Needed To Win.

I Can See Your Soul ◆

I Can See Your Soul

You're An Humble Mole

Looking For Someone To

Trust.

Someone To Have And To

Hold.just Like I Was Told.

Trust No One. Everyone

Might Be Looking For Gold.

So They Overlook The True

Diamond ◆ That's So Bold.

Yes I Can See Your Humble Soul.

Don't Cry For Me ◈

I Am A Freelance Bird

I Help When I Can

This's Not Hard.

I Come And Go As I Please

It Must Be The Freedom

Who Prepare My Meals.

On This Beautiful Land.

Every Family Create A

Diamond ◈. Key ⚷.

Don't Cry For Me.

The Door  Is Diamond

Too. So See Me Could Be

Your First Clue.

No Pressure To Change ♦

No Pressure To Change Who I Am.

I Am Already Set In My Ways

With A Lot Of Experience.

Search Your Soul

Curve Your Conscience

Its Okay If Your Thoughts

Are Up In The Air.

My Dna Is Lined With

Diamonds ♦ But Someone

Always Step In With Their

Own Vibes. Then This Space

Is Wide Open Under Your

Eyes. No Pressure To

Change. I Already Know Who I Am.

An Earth 🌍 Angel.😊

With Glamour.

Peace Of Mind ◆

Open My Mind To Be Free

Keep Me Sheltered For Me

Know My Ways, Let Me Be Me

No Need To Restrict You For

Restricting Me.

Smile Because This Note Is Free.

Peace Of Mind In A Diamond

World Is Not Easy.

Escape In A Thought Of Your Own.

That's Peace Of Mind To Me.

Strong And Bold.

DIAMOND BIRTHDAY ◆

Give Me Love

Top It Off With Some

Money Honey.

Give Me Gifts

Where Are The Flowers

Create It To Look Funny.

Give Me A Moment With

My Friends And Family Tree

Faith And Grace Can

Come With Me, Lets Eat.

Love Me Without Judgement

On My Birthday

Make Me Smile All Over Again.

Give Me Diamonds ◌

◆ To Blend In With This Poem.

Yay To My Diamond ◆ Birthday.

Have No Fear Everyone

Is Invited The Same Time Next Year.

We'll Do It All Over Again.

◆◆◆◆◆◆◆◆◆◆◆◆◆

GIFTED ANGEL

The World Is Round

What If I View It Directly

From Your Point Of View.

What If I Leave

This Thought 💭 Here.

I Wouldn't Feel Like

I Have A Mind Of My Own.

What If The World 🌍 Has No

Dimension Who Would

Know The Difference.

Just A Moment To Figure

This World Out.

It's Not A Gift To Have Your

Free Opinion. But It's A Gift

To Be A Gifted Angel.

Welcome 🎧 This Diamond💎

Page Is A Peek At My

Freedom. Gifted Angel 😊.

DON'T DIVIDE ME 💎

Don't Divide Me

I Am One Person

Don't Restrict Me

I Am A Free Will

Don't Doubt Me Or

I Will Always Win

Accept Me For Who I Am.

One Imperfect Person

Please Don't Divide Me

I Am Nothing Witout Jesus.

True Diamond Gives Love. 💎

Flaws Are Everywhere.

Just Show That You Care.

Don't Divide Me.

Please Dont.

FAMILY DIAMOND

Plant A Diamond In Every

Family. Just View It As A Tree.

The Pressure Of Life Will

Not Fit In. Just Believe And

You Shall Receive. Caption

The One That's Different.

Nuture And Watch It Grow.

Family Is A God Sent.

Blessings Are From Heaven.

Read This Note Over Again.

You're A Family Diamond

This I Know.

♦ DIAMOND SLAVE ♦

Strong Is Your Journey

No One Can Take It Away.

Walking In Your Destiny

Long Time Coming.

Looking Up Daily

No Need To Look Down.

Fear Not My Dear.

You're Not A Clown

Oh I Must Say , Behave

You're Freely Chosen As A

Diamond ♦ Slave.

Get out of the Cave.

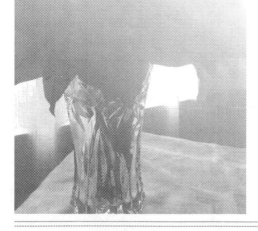

DIAMOND CROSS

Father God We Thank You

For Healing Our Souls.

We Thank You For Pressures Untold

We Thank You For Standing

By Our Sides Daily.

Father God We Thank You

For Your Love Kindness And

Mercies, Oh Glory Be To You
Father God.

What If An Outcast Created

A Diamond Cross.

What Would Be The Next Chapter.

Oh Father You Earn The

Diamond Cross, Not Whats

Leftover Help Us To

Bring More Lost Souls To

The Cross. We Need To

Prosper. Heal Every Soul.

Guide The Lost Home

With Their Diamond Cross

Oh Father God. Someday

Someday The World Will

See You As Their Only Cover.

Trust In The Lord Forever.

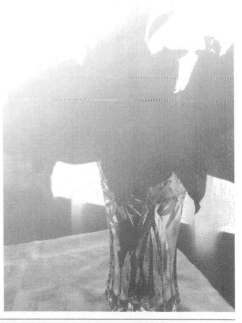

❖ JAIL BIRD DIAMOND ❖

Giving Up Hope Is A Waste.

Failure To Try Is Not An Option.

Courage And Bold Is On The

Front Burner. Don't Start

Lying Under Pressure. Know

The Code Is Love ♥ Even If

All You Can See Is A Dove 🕊

Jail Bird Diamonds Are

Everywhere. Innocent One

In A Gurney. The Only

Medicine Is Praying

Together For Freedom.

For Every Jailbird Diamond.

Stay Strong.

THE HOMELESS DIAMOND

Don't Look Down On Him/Her

This Could Be You

Crippling By The Cold

Open Your Heart

Create A Window

Help Freely With Jesus

In Mind. Sooner Or Later The

Homeless Diamond Will

Cross Your Path Again.

Bringing Souls To Jesus.

Eating With His New Found

Family. Sweet Jesus, Sweet Jesus. ♪♪...

NAVIGATION DIAMOND ♦

Going Through Life

Feeling Alone.

Was Always Judge Wrongly

By The Unknown. Don't Worry.

You Will Never Be Alone.

Find Your Way In Shades Of

Grey. If You Really Want To

Enjoy This Flow. See

Navigation In The Form Of A

Rainbow. Beautiful

World Out There To See.

Why Not Own A Navigation Diamond.

Find Your Way Home. ♦

Navigation DiamondIs A King & Queen.

Yet Still Unknown.

RAINDROPS PROMISES 💎

Raindrop Promises

Your First Clue.

Rainbow 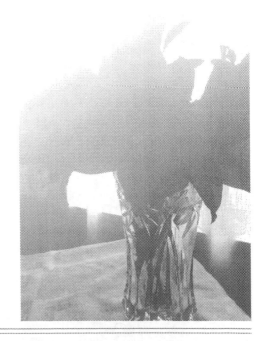 Wishes

Well Hello To You.

Cry Me A River Oh Bro.

Raindrop Promises Is

Blessings For Sure.

Sunlight Darling

Looking My Way

Diamond 💎 For You

Could Be Your Second Clue.

Love Means Freedom In

A World Of Raindrop

Riches. You Will Need

A Bucket To Recap This.

Now Open This Door ▌.

On Your Blessing.

DIAMOND MARBLES ◆

Flip This Diamond

Bring Back Old School

Real Friends Just Having Fun.

The Stake Is High This Game

Could Earn You A Real

Diamond. Flick You Marbles

Be Creative.

The Closest To My Heart Wins.

Diamond ◆ Marbles

Luxury In Every Country.

Poor Child Past Time.

To Unwind.

Make A Circle O Now Play

With Your Diamond ◆ Marbles.

Fake It To Win It.

Create Your Fun Twist.

◈ DIAMOND GREEN BIBLE

The First Book Was My

Lifeline. When I Am In Shock

It Open My Eyes. Whenever

I Was In Doubt.

I Just Read A New Chapter.

My Daily Bread Came From

The Bible. Black Is Beautiful

But I Would Like To See A Green Bible.

Just Like Color Purple

One Prince Idea Lives On.

Create A Diamond Green

Bible In The Future.

Pray For Me.

My Diamond Book Buddy.

Healing Forever.

FUTURE LOOKS BRIGHT ◆

Learn From Your Mistakes

Keep God Close

Moment Of Silence When

One Impose.

Work From The Inside Out.

Diamonds Are A Forever Quote.

No Need To Crack Under Stress.

Future Looks Bright

Stay Focus, Always Do

Your Best. Bold And

Beautiful Fits You Well.

Help Others When They're

In Need. But Don't Tell.

Because Jesus Blessed Us Well.

So We Will Humble Ourselves.

DIAMOND ◆ VALLEY

Diamond Valley

Could Be A Challenge

For Me. Every Family Name

Is Diamond ◆ So I Place My

Name On A Tree.

Walking Poet's Tree Was Written By Me.

So I Won't Need A Colar

To Walk On Diamond Valley.

Every Little Dog I See Was Diamond Molly.

Anything Goes On Diamond Valley.

Free To Be Free With

No Struggle Bubble.

Extraordinary Was The

Popular Note. Pass It Around.

Create Your Own Valley

This Poetry Art Is Worth

Money.

On Diamond Valley.

It's Okay To Be Silly

On Diamond Valley.

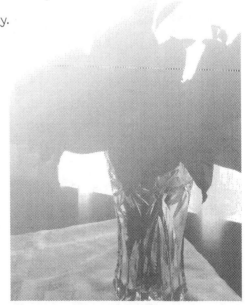

RECIPE FOR FRIENDSHIP ◈

2 Cups Of Patience

1 Heart Full Of Love

2 Handfuls Of Generosity

1 Dash Of Diamond For Laughter

2 Cups Of Loyalty

1 Cup Of Understanding

Mix All Ingredients Well.

Sprinkle Generously Over

A Lifetime And Serve To

Everyone You Meet.

Add Your Own Ingredients

Renew This Friendship

Over Again.

RISE BEYOND

Rise Beyond Your Imagination

Its Okay To Jump Skip

Or Swim For Diamonds

Give Your Best At All Times

Still Expect To Be Asked Why.

Practice What You Preach

Be Strong Not Weak

Live The Life That Best Fit

Your Suit. Beyond My

Wildest Dream Works For

Me.

Rise Beyond My Imagination

Helps Me To Feel Free.

Giving Is Everything.

Can't You See.

Rise

Rise

Rise.

Rise Beyond This

Notification.

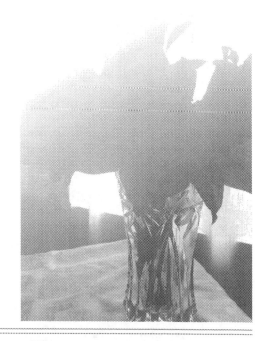

STRESS NOT ◈

Stress Not

Faith Comes First

You're A Gift And Not

A Diamond Curse.

Everyone Has Problems

Use Yours To Change The

World. No Stress Needed

On The Family Lawn.

Only Love Lives Here

No Need For Drama.

Now It's Time For Dinner.

We Will Revisit This Again

Tomorrow.

Stress Not My Dear.

Just For Tonight

Seek Refuge At

The Stress Not Factory

It's For Our Safety.

HAPPY DIAMOND ◆

Happy To Be Happy

I Can See That You're

Happy

Stay Happy

Look Happy 😊

Always Happy

Happy Happy 😄

Joy Joy Happy

I Can See Why You Will

Be My Happy Diamond

For This Blue Sky 🐦.

Twirl And Sing Along

Happy, Happy, Happy

Happy Bunny.

PRAY DAILY ⬦

Pray Daily

Prayer Heal Souls

Pray In Groups Or

Learn To Pray Alone

Jesus Is Still On The

Throne.

Pray Daily Feel Fresh

And Free.

Love The World In One

Diamond ⬦ Prayer 🙏

Cover Everyone With

Safety Prayer Daily.

Amen.

CONTROL YOUR ANGER ◈

Take A Deep Breath

Everyone Will Face This

Energy Someday. Study

Now So That You Will Be Prepared

For What Is Yet

To Come. Anger Is A Natural

Response When You Agree To Disagree.

Walk Away With

A Diamond Anger Someday.

Dance Around, Sing Along

Lets Get Physical In A Happy Way.

Control Your Anger Today.

Express This Over To Me.

Breathe In, Oh So Free.

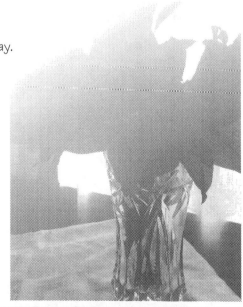

DOCTORS ARE HUMAN 2 ◆

Trust Your Doctors

But They're Not The Final

Say.

Love Your Doctors

Jesus Loves Them The Same

Way.

See Your Doctors When You

Can.

Doctors Needs Medication

Too. So Don't Be Mad When

Your Doctor Cannot See You.

Doctors Are Diamond Who

Needs Lawyers Too.

Smile And Say What!! A Jump.

From Drs Are Humans Too.

There's No Perfect Doctor.

Just Love Them All Before You Call.

Because There's No

Right Medication in This Chapter

Line This Note With Prayer

LAWYERS TRUTH ⬦

What If You Find A Laywer

Who Always Tell The Truth.

Would You Believe Yourself

Or Would You Caught Yourself In A Lie.

Just For Thinking This Thought 💭

Would You Trust A Lawyer

With No ⬦Credit Under His

Belt. Or Would You Trust

The One Who Would Lie

For His Client Himself.

Which Ever Angle You Plan To Use.

Trust The One Who Depends

On Jesus To Work It Out.

Choose!.

Now Pick Yourself Up

And Go To Court.

Welcome The Lawyers Truth.

It's No Hoax.

Pray Both Ways.⚖️

It's Going To Be Okay.

I LOVE CHRISTMAS 🎄

I Love Christmas

I Love Peace

I Love Happy Time

With Family Trees

I Love Jesus More

On This Day.

The World Celebrates

His Gifted Birthday.

My Smiles Gets Bigger On

Christmas Day.

Because Jesus Loves The

Gifted Me In Every Valley.

Diamond ❤ For Jesus On

Christmas Day Yay!!

Jesus I Got You Covered

On This Day. Because Every Other

Day You Thought Me How To Pray.

From The Core Of My Heart.

I Love Christmas.

I Hope You Love

Jesus The Same Way.

Hmm. Where's

My Diamond Dog Molly.

I Really Love Christmas

I am Trying To Find

Mr. & Mrs. Jolly.

MONEY WITHOUT DIAMOND

Mix Me Up

Twist Your Mind

Keep Me Close

With Your Kindness

Deep In Our Souls

We Can See Blindness

Open Your Eyes And See

The Light.

Talk About Anything

No One Will Be Rejected.

Diamond Without Money

Just Turn Things Around

With Laughter.

No One Pray How To Be A Pauper.

So Add A Line For

A Self Starter.

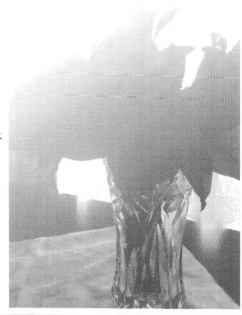

LAUGHTER IN ME.

You Tickle My Fancy

You Memorized Me.

You Feel Me Out

You Cover My Phase

You Know My Memo

You Search My Soul

Then You Sprinkle

Diamond Sparkles

All Over The Room.

You're The Soldier Who

Script A Unique Laughter In Me.

You Know That Apple

Don't Grow Under Trees.

Where's My Diamond Please.

Set It Free To Be Released.

Don't Forget To Squeeze

Me, Please.

DIAMOND RUBBER DUB DUB

Diamond Rubber Dub Dub

Love Baby Love

Give Me A Dubber Dub Dub

Rub Baby Rub Keep Me Close

With This Lover Love Love

Expect Only The Best

King And Queen Entering

This Chapter With

A Diamond Bed Rest

Passion For Life In My

Rubber Dub Dum.

With My Lover Love Love.

Rock Me To Sleep

In My New Hammock

For Keeps, Diamond To

Massage My Feet.

WHAT IF ♦

What if i am one of the wisest poet that ever lived.

What if i wore the dumbest dress without no zipper.

Would you be smart enough to cover me.

Or would you be laughing on the side line

asking everyone in the room

if they saw what just happened.

What if my English is not poetically correct.

Could you still see freedom of speech.

What if i don't care a damn

What you think of me.

Would you question my christianity.

What if i were you.

Could you still see me.

What if this poem makes

No sense would you read it to the end?

Then start over again.

♦What if ♦.

⬥ Flowers For You ⬥

This Special Moment

Is Long Time Coming.

This's Your Time To Shine.

You Own The World On

Your Birthday.

The Happiest

Day To Unwind.

Go And Spread Your Wings

Explore With Family And Friends.

Before You Go Into

Your Special Gift Wrap.

I Have Diamond

Flowers For You.

My Dear, I Love You.

This's Not A Clue

It's True.

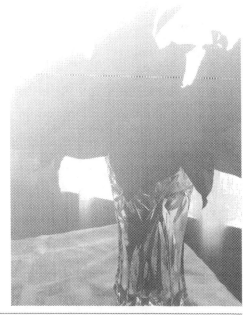

DIAMOND RAIN

Blessings ◈

Blessings ◈

Blessings ◈

Bless everyone

In the world oh

Lord.◈

Make it rain out of

The ordinary.◈

◈Diamonds falling from

The sky.

Oh Diamonds

Falling From The Sky.

Oh Lord Send Down

Your Powerful Rain.◈

No Need To Feel Insane

Make It Rain.

ANGEL DREAM ◆

The world will try to sway you like a swing.

Don't be afraid to listen to the squeak, ping.

Go back and forth and sway in the wind.

Diamonds are a girls best friend.

This knot is already taken.

Go deeper in your mental block

then welcome Diamond Brethrens.

When in doubt call on me.

I will give you wings.

Angel dreams like an angel

Now swingy swing swing.

Call Out The Name

Samuel.

You Are Not Alone.

Marriage Is Sacred ◈

Give this lifestyle time to breathe.

You're now one.

Marriage is sacred

It's Jesus theme.

You're talking to two people.

But your scope should

View one.

Opposite attracts for a

Reason. We need each other

In all season.

Marriage is sacred the world knows this.

Just like a diamond ○ with

A twitst.

SHOW ME THE LIGHT ♦

Reveal to me your delight

Give me wisdom to manage.

Satan says demon

♦Jesus said diamonds ♦

Why do we judge so easily

Where is the test that we pass daily.

There's no perfect note

Show me the light 💡 to

See wisdom through

the lenses of the wise one.

Who will welcome me.

Leave your doubt

Under the tree

Now I see you can.

SHELTERED CHILD ◇

To That Sheltered Child

Little By Little Learn To

Fend For Yourself.

Take Bits And Pieces And Put

Them Together Again.

Use Silent Moment

As Your Inspiration.

See Security In Your Blanket

Make Jesus Your Best Friend.

Smile In Every Moment

Put This Together Again.

This Time Around Create

Your Own Diamond Poem◇

Look Around Know Your Friends.

There's A Valley In Your Family.

Look Toward The Mountain ▲ For◇.

♦HOLY BELL♦

Find Peace In This World

To Be A Holy Bell Is Not A Sin.

Ring When You Need

To Call My Name.

Be Patient In Every Hour

Humbleness Is A Virtue

Not A Tower.

Faith Is Your Shield And

Your Cover.

To Push Things Further.

Be A Diamond ♦ Humble

Peaceful Bell.

With A Ring To It.

You're Blessed.

♦Loyalty Buddy♦

Stand beside me in the storm

Stay beside me in the struggles

Picture us hanging by

a diamond thread.

Holding us up is our love

and loyalty for each other.

No need to deliver gossip

It has no value.

Draw me closer honey

You're my loyalty buddy.

Forever bonus true loyalty ♥♦

♦DIAMOND BABY♦

The difference in culture

Gave us room to play with words.

In Jamaica you would be the wash belly

In America you're considered the last child.

In most paintings both could earn the same ratings.

It's like knowing a gifted poet who favors oprah.

Then you find yourself lost in this note 📝

my next move is to loan you a quote.

I was once a wash belly

But i am a invisible diamond baby.

Smile beyond your

Understanding of this

Poem. Holy Brethren.

DIAMOND FIRE

The future is going to be bright.

The young minds will be more creative.

Let see what they would do with diamond fire.

Setting the stage for the highest creative power

Lets see who could work

Under pressure then

Deliver the most magical moment to remember.

Look beyond the stars for diamond fire

Look deep within your dreams for sparks

Pull out the last passion

Now explore in your world.

Diamond fire is just a theme

Don't burn me. Set me free.

See the winner in thee.

DIAMOND MOLLYVILLE

My moment of silence

My peace of mind.

A place to escape and unwind.

A gifted dog who would

Never leave my side is now

In Mollyville heaven.

Memories lives on forever

True love will never die.

Flowers will always be

Close by. Molly memories

Will live on.

She was the apple of my eye.

Oh yes she was my Mollyville diamond

One of a kind.

Precious than gold.

True loyalty in control

At diamond Mollyville.

#Pwow

#Pwow.

Heal my soul at Mollyville.

❖ Super Bowl 2020 ❖

Everyone is waiting to read

this super bowl poem.

Including you

at the grandstand waving.

Who is this goofy spooky poet

with diamond wings.

Talking about super bowl

like an African queen

Locking her body and

Releasing her brain to pull

Out the winner. This's insane.

Patriots and steelers are

Out and about. Plug in your

Favorite team. Like a scout.

Cheers for our diamond ❖ fans.

Only winners will win one 🏈

Superbowl 2020 is open

Wide. No need to commit myself.

I love freedom it's an open book.

Touchdown sunday.

Say hi to the mvp cooks.

DIAMOND TEARDROPS ◈

Diamond teardrops

It's okay to cry

Diamond teardrops

It will be hard to say goodbye.

Diamond teardrops

This could be a lullaby

Happy moments forever

Look up in the sky.

Search your soul and free your mind.

Take in deep breaths and

Be kind. Diamond teardrops

Oh please be mind.

Because it's okay to cry ◈

Sometimes.

Sometimes I feel

Like a diamond teardrops.

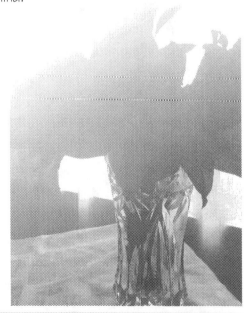

Diamonds Not Demons ⬙

Diamonds not demons

Masterpiece is in your name

Don't be a star 🪀 because

You're a diamond by far.

Believe in yourself

Don't be botch

You're the original diamond ball ⚽.

Climb the mountain ▲

Build up your strength

Diamond not demons

Wants to attack your health.

Stay focus and always wear

your extraordinary belt.

Like a diamond deep in the cave.

Smile, twirl and do your beauty wave.⬙.

Gifted diamonds for sale.

Just keep it real.

◆ DIAMOND ◆ FACEBOOK

The one book that's open wide.

Everyone has problems

Some pretend not to feel this way inside.

Then i look in the mirror

Without a judgment map

I wrote many poems with room for a gap.

To leave this world is not

Easy. But it's social enough

To accommodate all.

Read into everyone phone call.

Protect yourself from scope and spaces on top.

With every magnifying glass in hand.

Take a stand.

Give credit to facebook diamonds.

Love and respect to all my facebook friends.

This's real life, there's no competition.

Live your life the way that's pleasing.

Facebook is a open book 📖

Not everyone is gifted to keep on flying.

Like a kite diamond with wings

show me love.

Then raise you hand

with no gloves.

♦DIAMOND TWITTER

This Social Media operates

in a silent zone.

Operation x is all over the place.

With no abiding city.

Diamonds are welcome

this's one nation

with a fallopian tube to control.

Look deep in every bowl.

Hearts body and souls

Dancing under one diamond roof.

Leave me a knot to welcome the rain.

Twitter diamonds can be insane or real.

Fun to be me free with no pressure

Send me a seal for my

Silent behavior on ♦

Twitter.

Create a diamond

Bell for marketing.

◆ SOMEDAY ◆

Someday you will welcome a poetry bus

Around the bend call a poetry taxi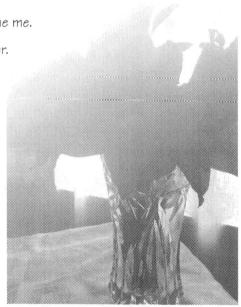

The world is not perfect

But we can create and learn to curve it.

Only love will benefit for it all.

Hatred and doubts are

struggling to cross over.

Diamonds ◆ for everyone

No matter, only love can

Prosper. Someday you will welcome me.

My heart will repeat with no anger.

Hmm someday ◆.

Poetry, poetry forever.

♦ DIAMOND WORLD ♦

It's okay to be different

Diamonds are at the border.

Diamonds are over the walls.

Diamonds are between-barriers

Its in the cross fire when you call.

Please don't crack under pressure.

Plug the strong will survive.

Give freely this's a circle O

Stay safe and alive.

You're a world diamond ♦

Turn your life around.

Strive for success.

Do it in a circle.

✧ ENJOY EVERY SEASON

Enjoy every season

Even if you're not where

You wanted to be.

Enjoy every diamond daily

Work with the angels freedom

Welcome the Sun

Smile with the stars ✦

Make every moment fun in mars.

Enjoy every season

Embrace the trees

Give thanks for the rain

Write for Jesus please.

He knows you well.

Like the precious diamond ✧

that you are.✧

Everyday is blessed with

Flowers.

Just for you, imagine if this

Was your first clue.

Be happy in every season

I got you.For a reason.

♦ FAKE OR REAL ♦

Fake or real

Jesus loves us the same

Way.

No need to fit in any policy

Or round off things with a lie.

True love lives on forever

Diamonds follow too.

Why cry.

Be happy in every note

Don't be a billy goat.

Fake or real uplift

Daily diamond in prayer

That's base with only love forever.

♦♦♦♦♦♦😊♦♦♦♦♦☐4

CALLING ALL DIAMONDS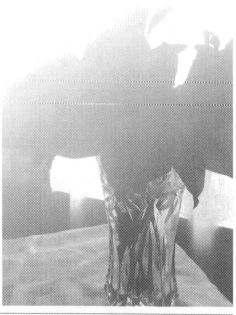

Calling All Diamonds

Calling All Homeless Diamonds.

Calling All Jail Bird Diamonds

Calling All Can't Pay

My Bills Diamonds

Calling Needing More

Help Diamonds.

Calling Give Me A Real

Job Diamonds.

Calling All Prayer

Warriors Diamonds.

Calling All Happy Diamonds

Calling Every Humble Diamonds

This Is The First Diamond Poem.

Let's See Why This Diamond

Make Sense.

Let's Uplift All Diamonds In

The World Today.

Rice And Poor Diamonds

Eating At The Same Table. Yes!

WORLD LEGACY ⬦

Wrap Up This Legacy

And Upgrade It.⬦

Don't Hide It

Or Throw It Away.⬦

Keep It Close To Your Heart

Open On Rainy Day⬦

The Core Of Every Soul

Should Be Love ♥⬦

Some Scope Up

Silver And Gold.⬦

Wave Your Hands

For The Real Diamond Fold.

This Legacy Will Make It

Happen Someday.⬦

Father God Forever Legacy

Is Always To Uplift And Love

Others No Matter Where🌍

They're In Life.⬦ ⬦ ⬦ ⬦ ⬦ ⬦

Like A Diamond ⬦

Our Legacy Will Lived

On Forever.⬦

DIAMOND CHEQUE ♦

I Asked Jesus This Question
What Should I Do With This
Royalty Check ♦
He Said My Dear
Put It Away For
Mr Rainy Day♦
The World Will Someday
Believe Your Story.
Plant This Diamond ♦
I Will Create True Wings.♦
This's Not Royalty
It's For Your Loyalty.♦
Giving Up
Was Never An Option.♦
Even When Stumbling Block
Set Stage.♦
Be My Guest,
With This Diamond Cheque.♦
All Debts Will Be Erased
For Everyone In This Room.
$1.01 Plant This Diamond ♦
Is Reality For A Gifted Poet.

DIAMOND EYE 💎

When You Don't

Feel Like A Star ★

Don't Be Fooled.

You're Not A Star ✴

You're A Diamond 💎

With a Few Scars.

Trusting Works

Better On Mars.

Drink And Party All You Want To.

This Diamond 💎 Eye 👁

Will Not Always Party With You.

Let's Twirl When You Can See Diamonds ♦

💎 In Your Own Eyes.

Yes!! Writers Do Write.

Diamond 💎 With A Little

Twist. Twirl But Don't Fall

Down. Hi 👋 Miss.

Can You See My Diamond 💎 👁 Eye.

✦ DIAMOND DREAM ✦

Diamond ✦ Dream

Could Create Havoc.

Give Answers To Things

That Don't Even Happen Yet.

Eyes Wide Open

Then Spin The Head Set.

Remix In The

Form Of A Poem

The World Takes Notes

To Swing On Their Front Lawn.

Everyone Holding A Copy

Of Plant This Diamond ✦

Smile Because I WIll Be

Passing Through Someday.

To Read Diamond Dreams

Do Come Through 🎧✦🔋

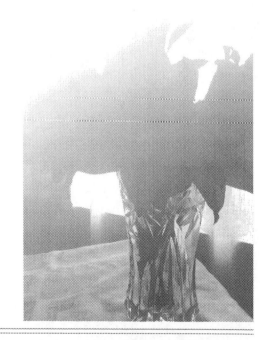

DIAMOND ⬦ BOB MARLEY ⬦

Bob Marley Wrote The

Diamond ⬦ Song One 🎸 Love.

I Will Uplift With One 🎸

Diamond ⬦ Like A Dove 🕊

Two Born Jamaicans

Shares A Note In Dreams

This World Will Never Forget

The One 🎸 Who

Makes Them Scream.

One Love Now Welcome One

Diamond Heart.

To Separate Us Is Too Far Apart.

One 🎸 ♥Love One

Diamond ⬦ One Gear.

Drive This V8 In The Future

With diamond ⬦

Bob Marley.

Live on forever 🎸♥🎸

I REMEMBER YOU

I Remember You

From The Corner Of My Eyes

I Remember You.

You Were In Deep Disguise

I Remember You

You Were My Event Planner

You Saw The Stars In My

Eyes So You Created A Winner.

But In My Mind

You Are The Winner

You're The Smooth Operator.

You're the Vim To My Vum

Sweet Diamond Pressure.

I Will Remember You

Forever. ♪♪

Forever ♪♪

You're A Winner A Winner

Show Me The Banner.

Oh Lord I remember you.

◆ DIAMOND BOSS ◆

The One That Will

Not Abuse Their Power

The One That Knows

The Empathy Code

Love And Think Of Others.

This World Might Not Be

Gold.

The Diamond Boss

Will Make Room

For Others

See Improvement As A

Stepping Stone.

Build An Empire

From Scratch.

True Happiness

Works Here

With A Diamond

Boss For The First Clue.

Everyone Feels

Truly Appreciated

When You Walk

In The Room.

Positive Effect

From A Diamond Boss.

KEEP ON TRYING

Keep On Trying

Never Give Up

Keep On Setting

Your Goals.

Work Under Pressure

If You Have To.

This Can Only Make You

Stronger.

Keep On Doing What You're

Doing.

You Will Never Walk On Stone Alone.

Set Your Mark On The World.

Like The Diamond That You

Are. Fun filled with happy memories.

All Learning Experiences.

To Share And Uplift Someone Else.

❤There's One Diamond ❤ The Entire World 🌍 Is Waiting To Meet.

This could be you❤❤❤❤❤❤❤❤❤❤❤❤❤❤❤❤❤❤

Printed in the United States
By Bookmasters